SHIRLEY ISHERWOOD

MIRACLES, WHALES AND WONDERFUL TALES

Voices from the Bible

Illustrated by
REG CARTWRIGHT GARETH LUCAS LIZ PYLE
ALLISON REED MEGAN STEWART

WATERLOO PUBLIC LIBRARY
HUTCHINSON
LONDON SYDNEY AUCKLAND JOHANNESBURG

To my dear friend Donald Loyd Hudson
for his constant support and encouragement

MIRACLES, WHALES AND WONDERFUL TALES
A HUTCHINSON BOOK 0 09 176869 1

Published in Great Britain by Hutchinson,
an imprint of Random House Children's Books

This edition published 2002

1 3 5 7 9 10 8 6 4 2

Text © Shirley Isherwood 2002
Illustrations © Reg Cartwright, Gareth Lucas,
Liz Pyle, Allison Reed and Megan Stewart 2002

The right of Shirley Isherwood, Reg Cartwright,
Gareth Lucas, Liz Pyle, Allison Reed and Megan Stewart
to be identified as the author and illustrators of this work
has been asserted in accordance with the
Copyright, Designs and Patents Act 1988

RANDOM HOUSE CHILDREN'S BOOKS
61–63 Uxbridge Road, London W5 5SA
A division of The Random House Group Ltd

RANDOM HOUSE AUSTRALIA (PTY) LTD
20 Alfred Street, Milsons Point, Sydney,
New South Wales 2061, Australia

RANDOM HOUSE NEW ZEALAND LTD
18 Poland Road, Glenfield, Auckland 10, New Zealand

RANDOM HOUSE (PTY) LTD
Endulini, 5A Jubilee Road, Parktown 2193, South Africa

THE RANDOM HOUSE GROUP Limited Reg. No. 954009
www.kidsatrandomhouse.co.uk

A CIP catalogue record for this book is available from the British Library

Printed in Singapore by Tien Wah Press [PTE] Ltd

CONTENTS

VOICES FROM THE OLD TESTAMENT

VOICES FROM THE NEW TESTAMENT

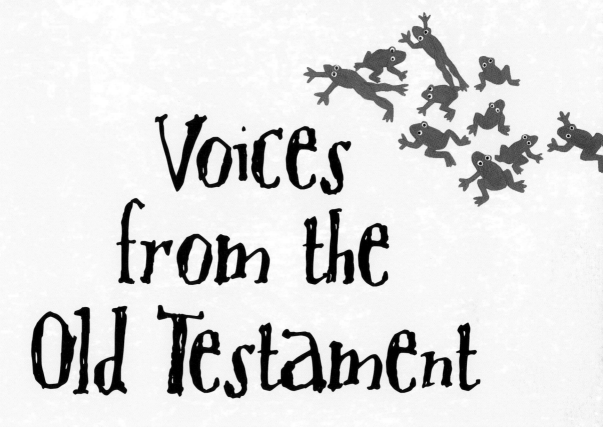

Voices
from the
Old Testament

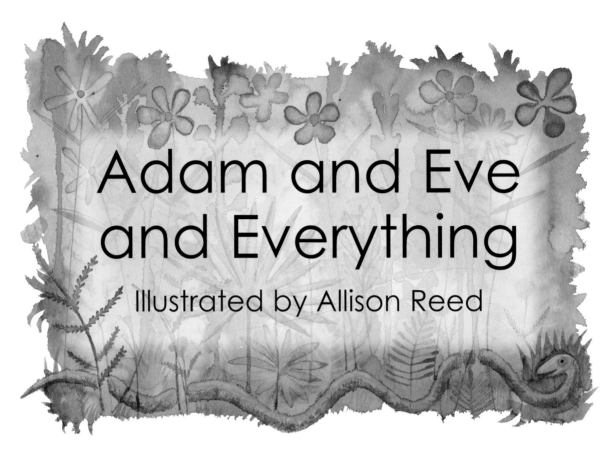

Adam and Eve and Everything

Illustrated by Allison Reed

In the beginning, there was nothing.

But, how can you imagine nothing? Even if you close your eyes tight-shut you know that you are still there. So, there is always something.

But there *was* nothing until God changed all that.

I think it must have been like it is when you are fast asleep, and not even dreaming. Then, you wake up and there's the world and everything in it that you like. And some things that you don't like so much! And there's the sun shining in through your bedroom window, because light was the very first thing that God made.

Or perhaps, when you wake, the rain is beating against your window, for water was the second thing that God made.

He made vast oceans and seas, deep lakes, rivers, streams and brooks. Brooks are gentle little streams and God made a lot of them. They ran along fields and meadows and through woods, so that all the creatures that he intended to make would always have something to drink.

Then he made plants: trees, flowers of every colour, and waving grasses, to give grain. He made the golden sun for daytime, the silver moon for night, and a whole universe of stars.

In the waters he made fish. Some were silver and some were gold. Some were so small they flickered through your fingers when you plunged your hand into a pond. Some were very large, and some lived so deep in the ocean that no one knew that they were there.

Well, God knew, and thought it would be fun when people discovered them too. They would be a wonderful surprise.

After he had made the fishes, God made the birds. He made big birds, like the ostrich, and tiny ones, like the humming bird, and all kinds of shapes and colours of birds in between. He made birds that sang, birds that called, and even birds that could copy human speech.

"And now, for the animals!" said God.

Oh, there seemed to be no end to the animals he could make – animals that ran and leapt, animals that climbed, that burrowed. Animals that liked to live together like families, and animals that preferred to be alone. Animals that roared.

Animals that bleated, neighed, grunted, barked, and purred. Animals that were striped, animals that were spotted, animals with thick fur, animals with sleek coats. He set them down on the earth and they ran through the fields and woods.

Some animals liked to live in places that were hot, and so he made jungles and rain forests. Some animals liked the cold, and so he made places of snow and ice. Some liked to live on the edge of the sea. Some were wild and fierce, and some were gentle and gazed at God's beautiful world with patience; for they were the animals that knew that there was something else to come – they were the animals who would learn to live with humans.

"And now, I will make humans," said God.

He made a beautiful garden in a place called Eden. And then he made Adam, and set him on his feet.

Adam looked around him, at the trees, at the plants, at the sky above his head where the birds flew. Like the gentle animals, he too knew that there was something else to come.

"I will make him a companion," said God, and he made Eve and set her beside Adam.

It was then almost the end of the seventh day. The sun was setting and it was a beautiful sunset. The sky turned purple and scarlet and gold.

Adam and Eve sat together and gazed in wonder.

But there was something missing, thought God – some little thing that was pretty and amusing, something to make you end the day with a smile.

It was a firefly; a creature so small it can scarcely be seen, except when it dances in the last beams of sunlight and makes a tiny fleck of gold.

Eve turned to Adam and Adam turned to Eve and they smiled at the sight.

God smiled too.

And so did I.

I lay coiled round the branch of the apple tree. The fruit hung all about me, round and red.

The tree held the knowledge of good and evil.

I knew this, but Adam and Eve did not. They were wandering about the garden. I heard their cries of delight when they discovered the beautiful things that God had made.

God let them wander and look and then he spoke to them. "The garden is yours," he said. "You may live here in peace and happiness, for in it I have placed everything that you will need."

My smile grew wider as I listened.

"You may do whatever pleases you," said God, "but you must not eat the fruit from this tree."

Adam and Eve turned to look at the tree, and I snatched up my tail, the tip of which I thought might be seen hanging below the branches.

Then I thought, But what does it matter if they do see the tip of my tail? Hasn't God just told them that he himself has placed everything in the garden?

Still, cunning told me, Do not show yourself just yet. Let them see things, let them learn things, let the feeling of greed, the desire for more and more grow in them.

Cunning it was that made me into a serpent. A serpent may slither silently through the grass and not be seen or heard. A serpent may lie, as I lay, coiled into twenty rings round a branch, so still that he might be part of the tree.

And so, I lay and listened to them as they roamed like happy children.

Eve loved the flowers best of all. She went from plant to plant, gently touching their petals and smelling their scent. And again, my cunning spoke to me. It said, she is the one, the one who can be tempted. The apple from this tree is the thing that will trap her.

And Adam? He was still playing a sort of game that God had made for him. God had not named any of the creatures. So, he had brought them to Adam to stand before him. And, one by one, Adam named them.

Listening to this, I almost weakened – the names were so right, as though the creature had always had that title.

"Rabbit!" said Adam. "Antelope! Dove! Dormouse!"

Oh, that last name almost undid me! But cunning is strong, and just at that moment, Eve came to sit beneath the tree.

I slid down the trunk and whispered into her ear, "Eve . . . Eve . . ."

She turned her head and looked at me. "How beautiful you are!" she said.

I *am* beautiful, with my green and gold scales; I twisted so that the sun caught them. And while she gazed at me, I told her about the apples. As I spoke, I saw her hand reach up, and take the fruit.

"Bite it," I said. "There is so much here that you have seen, but there is so much more that you cannot see. Bite the apple and you will see all!"

She bit it, and I went laughing through the grass.

Eve gave Adam the apple to eat. That night, when God came to the garden, Adam and Eve were afraid. They tried to hide, but God knew what they had done.

Then God made them leave the garden. He set an angel with a sword of flame by the gates so that they could not return – I saw the light of the flames flickering through the grass, where I lay.

I heard them weeping as they left. And I heard Adam ask, "Lord, will the animals keep the names I gave them?"

God's heart softened a little at this and he said, "Yes, Adam, they will."

And so they do to this day.

Rabbit. Antelope. Dove.

And Dormouse.

Noah and the Flood

Illustrated by Liz Pyle

Noah was the great-great-grandson of Adam, the very first man on earth – well, he was more than just his great-great-grandson, but he had so many "greats" that it would be too difficult to mention them all! He lived a long time after Adam had been made, when the world was full of people and creatures. Every creature on the earth still carried the name that Adam had given them – including me, a dove.

One day God told Noah to build an ark, which is a kind of boat. Noah was a good man, and had always obeyed God's laws, so he said, "Yes, Lord," and went to find his three sons, Shem, Ham and Japheth.

Shem said, "Why? Why must we build an ark?"

Noah said, "The Lord has told us to do so."

Ham said, "Well then, how shall we build it?"

Noah said, "We must build it with cypress wood. And it must be enormous. And we must paint it inside and out with pitch, to make it waterproof."

I saw Ham and Shem glance at one another. But Japheth just took up his axe, and strode off to the forest.

Soon the sound of falling trees could be heard. At this, Ham and Shem also took up their axes and followed their brother.

When they had gone, Noah raised his head to the sky. "My sons and I will do as you ask, Lord – but why do you ask it?"

There came a great sigh in answer, like a strong but gentle wind. It stirred the branches of the trees where I perched. Then a voice spoke. It seemed to come from everywhere, from every plant and every stone.

"Noah," said God, "humankind has become so wicked that I must destroy it."

Poor Noah fell on his knees at this. "Lord," he said, "I know that we are not as good as we ought to be, but we do try, my wife and myself and my sons and my sons' wives . . ."

He would have said more, but God spoke again.

"I have seen that, Noah," he said, "which is why I have told you to make the ark. I will flood the entire earth, and no living thing will survive except you, Noah, and your family . . . and the animals."

"Animals, Lord?" said Noah.

"Yes, indeed," said the voice of God. "You shall take two of every animal with you in the ark. Also, everything needed for each animal's comfort and well being."

Noah looked amazed – but again, before he could say anything the voice spoke once more.

"Yes," it said. "Hay and straw, grain, fresh water . . ."

The list was very long. I never knew that there were so many different creatures and that they needed so many different kinds of food!

As the voice spoke, Ham, Shem and Japheth came from the forest and listened. They too knew that what they heard was the voice of God.

I watched Noah's family work hard after this. Day and night, they hammered and sawed, and the ark grew and grew. When it was finished, the animals began to make their way to us. They came without anyone calling to them, or going out to seek them. They came quietly, in pairs. No one snarled, or jostled his neighbour.

I sat in a tree and watched them climb the gangplank that led to the door of the ark. How beautiful they were, what colours they had, how big and strong they seemed. Would Noah want me – so gentle, small and slight?

I told myself that he would not, that I would see the ark sail away on the great water.

But as the last animals made their way, Noah looked up.

"Come," he said, "little one!" and I flew to his shoulder.

We entered the ark and the great door slammed shut.

Then the rain began. It rained for forty days and forty nights; I heard it beating against the walls. The great vessel rose and fell. The humans found it hard to keep on their feet; even animals with four feet fell and tumbled against one another. I was flung about the great dark vessel, as though I was flying in a high wind.

Sometimes, when I perched on Noah's shoulder, I could look through a tiny crack in the wood – but all I saw were high pitching waves, grey water, and a dark, angry sky.

And so we sailed on, animals and humans, hearing the constant sound of the wind and the rain – until suddenly, one morning, silence fell, and through this very chink there poured a golden shaft of light. At first it was tiny, just a speck of light, but then it grew until it turned my breast feathers to gold.

Slowly, slowly the waters began to go down. The ark came to rest on a mountain top. After many days, Noah took me gently in his hands and flung open a window. There was nothing to be seen but the water around us, but it lay calm and still.

"Fly, my dove," he said, and I spread my wings.

I flew for a long time. I flew until the ark was a tiny speck on the horizon – then it vanished from my sight. But still, only water lay before me.

Afraid, I turned and flew back.

Noah was waiting for me. He stretched out his hand and I settled on his wrist. "Nothing?" he said. "There is nothing?"

After seven more days, Noah sent me out again. But still I found nothing, only the great endless sea below me and the great endless sky above.

I was about to turn when I saw, far in the distance, the top branches of a tree. The water was going back – soon green land would be seen once more! My wings were tired but I flew on, determined to reach this tiny sign of life.

The tree was an olive tree. I plucked a leaf and it smelled so sweet. Noah, watching for my return, saw what I brought him. As I flew to the ark, I saw the family come to the window and wave. How happy they were – how joyous the animals, cooped up for so long without new grass or fresh air or the feel of the sun.

Soon all this would be returned to us.

After another seven days, Noah sent me out once more, and this time I could sense that something had changed. I flew and flew until I spied what looked like an island on the horizon, lush, green and glowing with new life and hope.

As I flew towards it I saw something appear which was so beautiful and dazzling that I almost faltered. A breathtaking slice of colour, stretching in a perfect arc across the sky.

It was then that I heard the voice of God once more:

"As long as the earth endures –
seedtime and harvest,
cold and heat,
summer and winter,
day and night
will never cease."

And I knew that each time I saw a rainbow, I would remember his promise and his words.

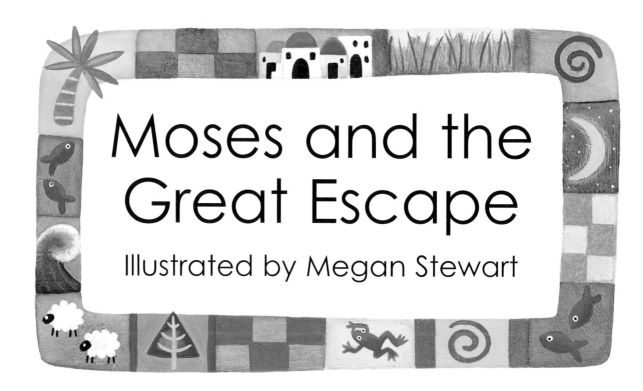

Moses and the Great Escape

Illustrated by Megan Stewart

My sister told me this story so many times when I was a child that I almost believed that I could remember what had happened to me. I thought that I recalled quite clearly the smell of the tar that coated my basket, the rustle of the reeds as my mother set me down amongst them, the white fluffy clouds that floated in the sky above my head, and the sound of the river itself.

Of course, I remember nothing – I was only three months old when it happened.

"A thousand years after the first ever rainbow, and four hundred years since we first settled in Egypt, God was still watching over us, his people – the Israelites," my sister would say.

"A new king came to rule Egypt, a powerful pharaoh, and when he saw how many Israelites there were, he became afraid. He said, 'If there are many more of them, then they could wage war against us. We will make them our slaves and if an Israelite woman gives birth to a boy then he must be thrown into the Nile, to drown.'

"When our mother heard this, she was afraid. She hoped that her new baby would be a girl.

"But you were a boy.

"Mother hid you as long as she could, and then she brought your little basket, put you in, and hurried down to the river. I followed her, and watched as she set the basket in the thick reeds that grew along the banks.

"For a moment she stayed, stroking your forehead gently, and murmuring, 'My baby, my baby boy.' Then she hurried away. But I stayed and watched as a beautiful young woman came down to the river with her servants.

"At that moment, you began to cry, and the pharaoh's daughter, for that is who the beautiful young woman was, knelt and parted the reeds and found you. As soon as she saw you, she loved you. 'I shall keep him!' she said.

"I was so happy then, to know that my baby brother would live," my sister would say, "but sad to think that I would never see him again. Then a wonderful idea came to me and I hurried to the pharaoh's daughter. 'Your highness!' I said. 'I know an Israelite woman who is very good at looking after small children.'

"'Send her to me,' she said. 'I will pay her to look after him.'

"And you lived with our mother until you were no longer a baby, when you went to live with the pharaoh's daughter."

So that is how I, Moses, an Israelite, was brought up as an Egyptian.

But I never forgot who I was, and when I was fully grown, I began to realize how badly the Israelites were treated by the Egyptians. They were made to work very hard so that they would not have the strength to rise up against the pharaoh.

One day, when I saw an overseer beating a helpless worker, I became so angry that I turned on the man, and killed him. Then, afraid that my crime had been seen, I fled to a country called Midian. There, I met and married the daughter of a priest. We had a good life, but I was always aware that I was a stranger in a foreign land.

One day, as I was watching my father-in-law's flock, I saw a strange and beautiful sight. It was a bush filled with flames. But while the bush burned, it stayed the same – there was no smell of charred wood, no branches fell to the ground.

Awestruck, I went closer, and heard a voice speak to me from the midst of the flames. It was the voice of God.

"I have seen the misery of my people in Egypt. I have heard them cry out. So go, Moses, to Pharaoh, and tell him that you are bringing the Israelites out of Egypt, to worship me."

What could I do but obey? I travelled back to Egypt and went straight to Pharaoh and told him what God had said; but the pharaoh refused to let the Israelites go.

At this, God grew angry and turned all the water in Egypt red with blood. Then he sent a plague of frogs. They were everywhere, in the fields and houses, even in the bowls where the Egyptians kneaded their bread. But still the pharaoh said that the Israelites could not go.

God then said to me, "Go before the pharaoh and strike your staff in the dust." I did as the Lord asked, and each mote of dust became a gnat. They filled the very air that the Egyptians breathed, but still the pharaoh shook his head.

After this came the flies. Then all the Egyptian cattle died and a plague of sores tormented the Egyptians themselves. As before, the Israelites were untouched by all this.

Next, the Lord caused a great storm to cover Egypt, but he did it in such a way that it did not harm the Israelites. They stayed safe, while the sky grew black as night, and hail stones as hard as iron flattened the crops in the fields.

Pharaoh's ministers hurried to him and said, "Can you not see that Egypt is being ruined?"

But he would not listen.

The locusts came then; they came in their millions. The land was black with their bodies and they ate everything that had been saved from the fields. They ate every leaf from every tree and every bush. Yet the trees and bushes of the Israelites remained green.

God then made the blackest of nights, which covered the land for three days. And then one night he sent a curse on the Egyptians that was worse than anything they had yet seen; not one Egyptian first-born child lived to see the dawn. But the Israelite families remained unharmed, passed over by God's wrath.

And so, at last, the pharaoh said that the Israelites could go.

I hurried to my people and we gathered our belongings together as quickly as we could – even the bread which was being made we took just as it was, without the yeast being added.

There were hundreds and thousands of us, with animals and children, and we left our homes in the dead of night and walked for days. The Lord sent a great white cloud to guide us. We rested in camps and then journeyed on, walking endlessly, day and night.

But the pharaoh regretted letting his slaves go and sent an army to bring us back. By now, we had crossed the desert, and had come to the edge of the sea.

"Lord," I said, "how are we to go on?"

"Raise your staff," he told me, "and hold it over the water."

I did as he asked. Suddenly, the sea parted, and a wide path lay before us. The waves just rose and then became still, as if frozen in the air.

I heard the gasps of astonishment from my people. "How can we walk through a sea?" they asked. "The waves will fall on us." So I took the first step, then turned and faced them. Behind, in the far distance, Pharaoh's army approached. I beckoned to my people, and after a moment's stillness, they followed me. The waves stayed like walls of glass on either side and sea birds flew and cried above our heads.

The cloud that had guided us now kept the Egyptians at bay, sending down great pillars of fire and throwing the army into confusion. But still they followed us into the great path that cut across the sea.

At daybreak we reached the other side.

And then the waves fell. They fell on the soldiers of Pharaoh's army and all were drowned.

We stood still, looking at where the path had been – shocked and silent as if unable to take it all in. And then I saw my sister pick up her tambourine, and there was great rejoicing in the desert.

But we never forgot the hardship that the Israelites suffered in Egypt, and how our Lord led us to safety.

Then God showed me the way to the land he had promised his people, a land flowing with milk and honey – a land we could call our own.

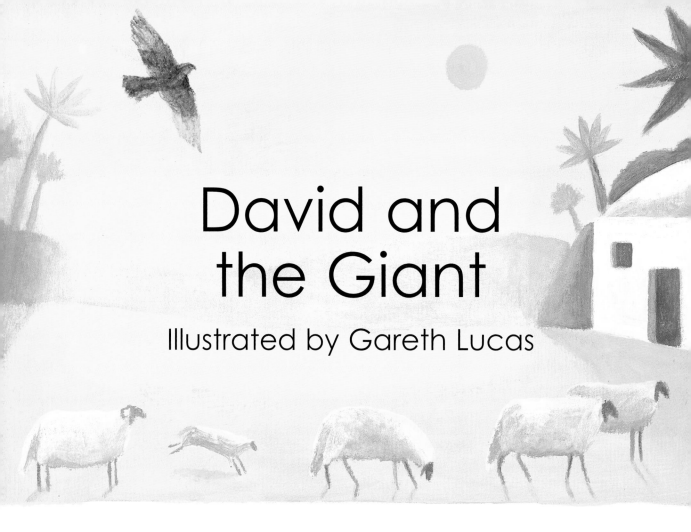

David and the Giant

Illustrated by Gareth Lucas

A few hundred years after Moses led his people to the promised land, the Israelites were in need of a leader, and this great king came from very humble beginnings.

David was a shepherd; he was also a harpist. The music he made echoed over the hills where he tended his sheep. He was a gentle boy and wanted nothing more than this. He was my youngest brother.

I am Eliab, and my story starts with the day my brothers and I were summoned by our father to meet the famous prophet, Samuel. Samuel was a great leader. It was he who had chosen Saul to be our king.

We were all excited by this honour, and even more so to discover that one of us was to be anointed by him with oil. I was the eldest, as well as the biggest and the strongest, and I told myself that the chosen one would be me.

But it was not me, nor was it any of my brothers who were with me. The youngest and smallest of us, away tending the sheep on the hills – he was the one. My father was told to send for him, and as soon as he came, Samuel said, "He is the one. The Lord has chosen him." I wondered, For what has he been chosen?

I was soon to know the answer to my question.

Soon after this, a war began between the Philistines and the Israelites, and my brothers and I went to fight as soldiers. But David stayed in the hills with our father's sheep, and did little but tend them, and play upon his harp.

Our camp was on a hill, as was the camp of the Philistines, so that the two armies faced each other with a low-lying plain between.

The Israelite soldiers were brave and strong, but the Philistines had a champion, a huge giant called Goliath. None would face him, and he strode from his tent every morning, dressed in his magnificent armour. For forty days he strode out, and called to the Israelites, "I defy the army of Israel!" But no one dared challenge him.

Then one day, to my surprise, my little brother David came into the camp, bringing bread for us, and cheeses for our commander. He wanted news of the battle to take back to our father.

Everyone crowded round David at this, to tell him about Goliath. "He stands there," they told him, "and cries out in a terrible voice, 'Give me a man and let us fight each other. If I die then the Philistines will become your subjects and serve you.' Then he laughs, for he knows that no man will come to stand against him."

"What will be the reward of the man who kills him?" asked my little brother.

"The king will give him great wealth," he was told. "Also, he is promised the king's daughter as a wife, and neither he nor any of his family will have to pay taxes ever again."

"And still no one has come forward?" said David.

I was angry at hearing these words. How dare the youngest and smallest of us, the keeper of sheep, the harp player, suggest that we were cowards! My brothers just laughed, but my anger remained – I had not forgotten how David had been anointed and I had not.

"You are conceited and wicked," I said to him, "and you have only come to watch the battle, like the coward you are. Go back and tend to your sheep – they are all that you deserve!"

David left shortly after. We thought that he had gone home, but we were wrong. He did not go home. We learned later that he had been to King Saul and had told him that he, David, would fight Goliath.

He returned to us on a day of sunshine and showers. He was dressed as he always was, in a tunic and a cloak, and carrying only his shepherd's staff and his leather sling. We were astounded when he passed us all by and stood alone at the brow of the hill, and called out, "I will fight Goliath!"

His voice echoed round the hills.

The Philistine camp was still and quiet, but at the sound of David's voice, tent flaps were thrown back, and men came forth. With them, came Goliath.

Goliath was nine feet tall. He was clothed in armour that shone in the sun. He carried a spear and a great sword hung at his side. His bearer walked before him, carrying a huge shield. What could my brother do against such a man?

David began to make his way down to the plain that lay between the two hills.

"Someone should stop him – he's only a boy!"

I heard these words all around me. But no one tried to stop him. Neither my brothers nor I tried. I cannot speak for my brothers, but I suddenly thought of David's anointing and told myself, it was for this – for this. And all the envy of my little brother vanished and I felt nothing but love.

But a desperate fear gripped my heart; my baby brother looked so small and defenceless, standing across from the armour-clad giant.

Goliath looked at my brother, then he raised his eyes to the hill where we all stood. "You send me a boy – a boy with a stick, as though I were a dog!" he shouted.

He turned his eyes on David then and said, "Come here, boy, and I will feed you to the birds of the air, and the beasts of the fields."

He raised his spear high, as if to throw it.

I heard my brother cry, "You come against me with shield and spear, but I come against you in the name of the Lord Almighty, the God of the army of Israel!"

As he spoke, he took a pebble from his pocket, put it into his sling, whirled the sling around his head and threw it.

It hit Goliath in the middle of his forehead. For a moment, the giant stood, as though nothing had happened. Then his spear fell to the ground, and slowly, he fell after it.

David ran to his side, took the sword and waved it about his head. The crowds were silent for a moment and then a mighty shout arose.

"He has slain Goliath, slain Goliath! He is a boy born to be a great leader – a great king!"

And a great king he became, my brother – the youngest and smallest of us all – who once slew a giant with a stone and a sling.

Jonah and the Whale

Illustrated by Reg Cartwright

My name is Jonah, and I am no warrior like that mighty soldier, King David, who lived so many years ago.

I am not a coward either, but one night I was wakened by the voice of God.

"The great city of Nineveh has grown very wicked," he said, sadly, "and I need a good man to go there and preach my words."

I was afraid. Anyone being woken in the night by the voice of God telling him to go and preach in an evil place would feel afraid.

So, I dressed as quickly as I could and ran away. I went to a place called Joppa.

What a fool I was to think that the Lord did not see where I went, that his voice could not reach me no matter where I hid.

At the port, I boarded a ship bound for Tarshish.

The Lord watched this, but said nothing. Instead, as soon as the ship was out at sea, he sent a great storm.

The sky grew black with great clouds and the sea heaved and tossed.

I knew nothing of this. I was so pleased to have escaped the Lord and his frightening commands, that I slept as though dead.

The captain came to where I lay, below decks. He prodded me awake. "How can you sleep?" he asked. "My crew are on deck, all praying to their gods – crying out to this god, crying out to that god – oh, so many gods! But none of them answer." He looked closely at me. "But you, Jonah, you sleep!"

He hurried me out onto the deck. The sailors were huddled together, muttering. They turned to look at me, then one came forward.

"None of us has committed any great sin," he said. "This storm is not a punishment sent by our gods. It must be a punishment sent by yours, so why should we suffer for your sins?"

But I have committed no crime, I thought.

"I am an Israelite," I said boldly, "and I worship the Lord of All Creation."

This seemed to frighten them, for they huddled back together. Then the spokesman said, "What must we do to please your god and end the storm?"

"Throw me into the sea," I said, "and the waters will be calm once more."

I do not know to this day why I said those words. I think that God put them into my mind and I uttered them at his command.

The sailors seized me and threw me overboard; at once, the sea grew calm. For a moment, looking up, I saw their faces gazing down at me with awe. Now they will believe in my God, I thought. I was glad about that, but I did not want to die for the sake of it! Then the waters closed over my head, I felt fronds of seaweed wrap round my shoulders, and I thought, The Lord has abandoned me.

Then, even as I had this thought, I felt the waters surge and lift around me. I saw a great creature swimming towards me.

"Lord," I said, "forgive my sins and save me from . . ."

The creature opened its mouth and swallowed me.

". . . the perils of the deep," I said, closing my eyes tight shut.

When I opened my eyes, I found myself in a kind of cave, a warm cave that seemed to throb gently in every part. I put my hands on the walls and felt the warmth. I heard the sound of something beat with a slow, steady pace.

I was alive, inside another living creature.

"Lord," I said, kneeling, "you have saved me and in return I will do anything you ask."

I waited then for an answer, but none came. Instead, I had the thought that the creature that had swallowed me must soon swallow something else. All creatures must eat. And when my creature ate, what then would happen to me?

But nothing happened. My creature did not eat. Time passed. I began to relax. I curled against the warm wall and listened to the sound of steady beating in my ears. I slept and woke, slept and woke, then slept and woke again; so I supposed that three days and three nights had passed.

And my creature sang to me; not a song with words but a song made of sounds that told of the sea, of day and night, the stars and moon, of mankind and all things living under the sun.

"Lord," I said, hearing this song, "I will preach your word."

As I spoke, my creature gave a great cough, and I was hurtled up and out into the fresh air and the morning light.

When I caught my breath, I stood on the beach, and saw, some way out to sea, the tail of my creature.

It flipped twice, as if in farewell.

Then she vanished, and I turned and began to make my way to Nineveh.

Voices from the New Testament

A Very Special Star

Illustrated by Gareth Lucas

Early one morning, Joseph came to my stable. "My donkey," he said, "we must go on a journey."

He scratched the top of my head as he spoke, and then he scratched my ears.

Joseph was a kind man, a gentle man, not a man who would beat his animal, or give it fodder kept too long in the bin so that it had a musty taste.

"The journey will be long," he said. "We have to go to Bethlehem to pay our taxes and write our names in a book."

I brayed loudly at this – I had often thought the ways of humans strange – but to go all the way from Nazareth to Bethlehem to write names in a book was the oddest thing yet.

"You may laugh," said Joseph, "but go we must, Mary and I. It is the law of the Romans who govern us, and we must obey."

He lifted the lid of the bin and the scent of the good fresh fodder caught my nostrils. He took some out, and for a while he watched me eat.

"Mary is having a baby," he said at last. "So you will be carrying not one but two."

Babies are small, I thought, munching. A baby won't make my burden much heavier.

"The baby is to be born quite soon," said Joseph. And then he whispered, "He is a special baby. You will have to tread with great care, my little one."

I snorted at this – spraying him with fodder. How many times had he seen me stumble? Never!

Joseph laughed and brushed the bits from his robe.

"But, you never stumble," he said.

That day we set out on our journey. We left early to escape the heat of the sun. At night, Joseph made a sort of tent from cloths hung over long poles, and we all three rested underneath. Mary sewed clothes for her baby. Joseph, who was a carpenter, carved a little wooden figure for the baby to play with when it was born.

Mary smiled at him. "It will be a long time before the baby can play with toys," she said. But Joseph just went on carving.

And so, stopping each night to rest, we made our long journey. One evening, I turned my head and looked back.

Oh, how big the wilderness behind us seemed, and how far we had come! The sight made me think how tired I was, how sore my hooves were.

And then I looked up and saw the star. I knew at once that it was a very special star. I knew too that Mary's baby was a very special baby, and that I must forget my sore hooves and carry them to Bethlehem as quickly as I could.

I wanted Joseph to look up and see the star too. I butted him gently with my head.

"What is it, my little donkey?" he asked. "Have I tied the bundle too tight?" He ran his fingers gently under the straps.

I thought, Perhaps it doesn't matter that he hasn't seen the star. Perhaps the star is not meant as a sign for Joseph but as a sign for someone else.

I wondered who it could be.

Early next morning, we came to Bethlehem.

As soon as we entered the town, my nostrils caught a thousand scents and my ears a thousand sounds. The streets were narrow, so narrow and so filled with people and animals that we could move neither forwards nor back.

"Joseph . . ." I heard Mary murmur, and knew from her voice that she felt uneasy.

People were jostling her on either side; I felt her being pushed first this way and then that.

I filled my lungs with air, and let out a great bray.

"My donkey!" said Joseph – and his voice told me that he was both surprised and amused.

The crowd about us was certainly surprised, for it parted and I trotted through.

We went about the town, but could find nowhere for Mary and Joseph to stay. Every inn was packed with travellers come to pay their taxes.

At last, an innkeeper took pity on us. "There is only my stable where my cattle sleep," he told us, "but you are welcome to stay there."

It was a nice little stable, the roof was low and the walls were of stone. Two cows with great gentle eyes stared at us. Their calves moved closer to their sides, but I don't think that they were afraid of us.

"At least we are all together," said Joseph.

He and Mary settled themselves on the straw and went to sleep. But despite the long journey, I felt wide awake. Outside, the city had fallen silent.

I went out but could see nothing, only the black shape of the buildings around and, above my head, the great star.

It had followed us. It had grown, and now it shone more brightly than ever. I couldn't tell the meaning of it. I stood and gazed at it for a long time. Then, as I stood I heard the cry of a baby.

I waited, and after a while Joseph came out to me.

"The baby is beautiful," he told me, "and we will call him Jesus. An angel came to me in a dream and told me that was to be his name."

Joseph went back to Mary and the baby. I turned to follow him as the great star shone in the sky.

It was only later that I came to know what the star was for. One night some tall, dark figures appeared in the courtyard, leading their camels.

"Little donkey," said one, "he is here, isn't he, the newborn king – the Son of God?"

I nodded my head meekly and led them in.

Oh, how they shone and glittered in the dim light of the stable! They were wise men from the east and their robes were woven with gold and silver threads. They held gifts for the baby and they knelt before him. I was not sure what some of the gifts were, but Mary was pleased with the beautiful pots and whatever it was inside that smelled so sweet.

But I knew what gold was, and saw Joseph smile. My Mary and Joseph had possessed little enough gold in their lives.

I stood quietly at the back of the stable with the cows and their calves.

I wished that I too could give the baby a gift. He looked so small and sweet, lying in his mother's arms.

Then I remembered our long journey, and how I had stood and gazed back at the long trail of my hoof prints in the wilderness.

But I brought them here, I thought. Me – Joseph's donkey!

After we had returned to Nazareth, I watched Jesus grow to a man. When I was an old donkey I went with him to the place where John the Baptist preached.

John was a great man, loved and respected, but when he saw Jesus approach him in the River Jordan, he told the people who had gathered round, "This is the man of whom I spoke! This is Jesus, the Son of God."

But I had always known that. I had known it since the night when he was born.

Fishes, Loaves and Miracles

Illustrated by Liz Pyle

My grandmother was making bread, thumping the dough down hard on to the table so that puffs of flour flew up like little clouds. I like to watch my grandmother making bread, but on that day I heard the sound of many footsteps and voices, so I hurried out to see what was happening.

A crowd of people was passing by our house. There were people wandering by on their own and there were family groups too, just like mine. I wondered where they were going.

Then I heard them talking about Jesus of Nazareth – the man who healed the sick and spoke about God's kingdom. They talked of the preacher John the Baptist too, and said that he had been killed. They said that Jesus was going to a quiet place in the hills with his closest followers, and they were going to find him.

I ran back home and told my grandmother this news.

She covered the loaves with a cloth as she listened.

"Everyone says that Jesus is a wonderful, gentle man," I said. "And that he can cure the sick. I wish I could take Zachary to see him."

My friend Zachary was lame and couldn't walk or run very well. He did walk and run, like the rest of the children, but it was hard for him, and he soon became tired. Then he just sat and watched us play. It made me sad to see this.

But my grandmother didn't believe what was said about Jesus. "Herbs are what cure, Joshua," she said. "Herbs cure fevers and all kinds of illnesses."

"They didn't cure Zachary's leg," I said.

"Some things you just have to put up with," she said.

My grandfather came into the house. He had been fishing and his net was packed full. He too had heard the people talking. We sat together at the doorway and watched the crowds pass by. It was plain that they had come a long way. Some of them looked tired, for they were carrying people on stretchers. But all were joyful. There were small children too, and babies in arms and older people who walked with a stick, or leant on the arm of a younger person.

Then Zachary came up to us. "They all sound so happy," he said. And there and then I decided what I was going to do.

"I'm going to take Zachary to see Jesus!" I said.

My grandfather nodded.

I went back into the house. My grandmother was dozing, but she opened her eyes and gave me a keen look.

"I want to go and take some bread to the people who are going to see Jesus," I told her. I said nothing about taking Zachary too.

"Five small loaves will be enough," she said and closed her eyes again.

"But there are a lot of people, Grandma," I said.

"Five," she said firmly.

"And some fish," whispered my grandfather, handing me two dried fish in a little cloth.

The hills on the other side of the lake were much further away than they had seemed. Many families and groups of people passed us, and many offered to carry Zachary.

His limp had become very bad but he refused all help. "I want to do it by myself," he said.

I was afraid that we would be too late to see Jesus and his followers, but at last we reached the place.

Thousands of people were there, and Jesus was moving amongst them, bending and speaking to each one. As he spoke to the ones who were ill we saw the look of pain leave their eyes, and the lines on their faces grow softer.

Some had been blind and could now see. They gazed round them with a look of wonder.

We stood and waited patiently until Jesus drew near. Then, just as he was approaching, he called his closest followers to him.

They were his disciples and I recognized some of them, as they had been fishermen at Lake Galilee, just like my grandfather. They all believed in Jesus and loved him.

"These people have been with me all day. You must feed them," Jesus said.

"We will give him the loaves and fishes," I whispered to Zachary.

Zachary gave me a look of scorn. "That won't feed thousands!" he said, and he was right.

The hillside was covered by a great mass of people.

But something told me that even though we had so little, Jesus would welcome it. I went a little closer to him, touched his robe to get his attention. He turned and gave us a glorious smile. His teeth were very white in his dusky face. Just to be near him made me feel happy. I held up my basket and Zachary held up the fish.

"It isn't much," I said.

"It is enough," Jesus told us.

He bent and laid his hands on our heads, and then he moved on. But I wanted to stay near him, if only for a little longer.

I tugged at Zachary's hand to follow, and heard him give a gasp of astonishment.

"Joshua!" he said, and I became aware that he was no longer moving in the awkward, jerky way in which he had always moved.

"Thank you, Jesus!" we called. "Oh, thank you!" and he turned his head and smiled at us once more.

Zachary and I sat and watched, dumbfounded, as Jesus broke the loaves and gave thanks for the food we had brought. Then his disciples began to move amongst the great crowd of people. All they had was the little basket of bread and the little bundle of fish, but somehow everyone was fed. Zachary and I were too.

"It is a miracle!" said an old lady, who sat beside me. I looked at Zachary and smiled – it was not the only miracle that had taken place that day.

Later, we made our way home, moving easily with the throng of people. All were strong and happy and excited, just like my friend Zachary. He ran and jumped just for the joy of it. Those round us smiled to see it. I smiled too. I carried the empty basket with the little cloth folded neatly at the bottom.

As I drew near to our house, I saw my grandmother waiting.

"Well?" she said. "Was it enough, as I said?"

"Yes, Grandma," I told her, "it was."

The Story of the Good Samaritan

Illustrated by Reg Cartwright

My name is Zachary, and I was lame and could not run and play like other children, until my friend took me to see Jesus. How wonderful it was, to be able to move easily, to jump, to beat my friend at a race – although he did not care much for that!

So when I heard that Jesus was going to preach at a place not far from where we lived I went to listen to him, and learn from him.

He didn't preach in the way that the old priests preached.

Sometimes it was hard to understand what they meant.

Instead, Jesus told stories, and answered questions from the crowd.

That day, a teacher stood up and asked Jesus, "What must I do to live a good life and please God?"

And Jesus said, "Love God with all your heart and love your neighbour as much as you love yourself."

"But who is my neighbour?" asked the man.

And Jesus told us this story:

Once there was a merchant who traded in silks and wools. His father did this before him, and the merchant hoped that when he grew up, his little son would be a merchant also; one day they would go together along the road that leads from Jerusalem to Jericho, but that day was far in the future.

The little boy thought that he was already old enough to make the journey. "Please, Daddy?" he asked, as he helped his father tie the bales to the mule's back.

"My boy," said the merchant, "the road is very hard and very dusty. It is also very long."

Then he kissed his little son goodbye and then he kissed his wife, Rebecca.

"Take care!" his wife whispered, handing him a skin of wine and some food for the journey. They both knew that travellers were often robbed on the road from Jerusalem to Jericho. But they said nothing of this to their little son.

And so the merchant set off. It was very hot and the road was dusty, so after walking for some time, the merchant sat down in the shade of some rocks for a rest. His mule stood patiently beside him.

Both man and mule had almost drifted off to sleep when the robbers struck. They came silently from behind the rocks, and the merchant knew nothing until he was seized and his cloak ripped away. The poor mule reared and cried out in fright. Two of the smaller bundles fell from his back.

The merchant was beaten with heavy sticks and cut with knives. He was thrown to the ground, and saw his mule and his bales of wool and silk dragged away. He turned his head and saw the wine that he had brought seeping into the earth. He saw also his own blood, making an ever-growing dark patch on the dusty ground.

Then, to his joy and relief, he saw someone making his way along the road. The merchant raised himself on one elbow, and called out, "Brother . . . brother!"

The man was a priest. He would help, the merchant felt sure.

But the priest passed by. He scarcely glanced at the merchant; the poor man might have been a bone or a rag lying there in the road. The merchant watched him for as long as he could, watched the swing and sway of his robes as he strode on. He said to himself, He will stop and turn, and hurry back saying, "Brother, I have only just realized what I have seen!" That was it, the merchant told himself – the priest's mind was so full of his duties, all else was blotted out.

But the priest did not stop and turn.

The merchant fell back on the ground, and curled up like a baby.

He had no idea how long he lay like this before he heard the sound of someone's footsteps on the road.

He raised himself up again, and cried out weakly.

The passer-by was a Levite – a religious man. The merchant saw that from his robes.

He thought for a moment that the Levite had not heard, and cried out again.

This time he knew that his cry had been heard, for the Levite's head turned slightly. Then his eyes fixed on the road before him again.

"You are a man of God!" the merchant shouted.

But the shout was only in his mind. The sound he made was as faint as that of a newborn kitten.

The merchant fell back again.

He thought of his little son and of his wife Rebecca.

She would be weaving, and his boy would be dreaming of the time when he would tread the long trade road with his father.

That will never happen now, thought the merchant.

He drifted into a kind of sleep, and was awakened by the touch of someone's hand under his head.

"Drink this, brother," said a gentle voice, and a cup of wine was put to the merchant's lips.

The merchant revived enough to see that the man was a Samaritan, of all people! Why would a Samaritan want to help him? They had different beliefs, different ways of living. They were supposed to be enemies.

But the Samaritan bound the merchant's wounds and stopped the bleeding. Then he poured oil on his bruises. He took the bundles from his own mule's back, and helped the merchant to mount the animal. The heavy bundles were slung over his own back.

And so the three made their way to Jericho.

Sometimes the merchant lay, half-sleeping against the mule's strong neck, sometimes he tried to speak, to thank his rescuer.

But the Samaritan just said, "Don't talk – rest."

He took the merchant to an inn, where he was given a comfortable bed. The Samaritan looked after him, and when the merchant had recovered he told the innkeeper that he would return soon and pay what he owed.

But the innkeeper just smiled and shook his head. "You owe me nothing," he said. "The Samaritan paid before he left."

The merchant set out on the road home, thinking joyfully of Rebecca and his little son. He thought too of the Samaritan. I owe that man my life, he said to himself, and I don't even know his name.

After Jesus had finished his story he turned to the teacher and said, "In your opinion, which of those three men was a good neighbour to the merchant?"

"The Samaritan," he replied.

"Go and be like him," said Jesus.

And so we made our way home.

I thought, I will always try to be what Jesus wants me to be. I looked for someone fallen on the way, set upon by robbers and beaten – but there was no one, everyone was well and happy.

But I knew that someday someone would need me, and that I would be there to help them, whoever they were.

The Last Supper

Illustrated by Megan Stewart

I remember that day as if it were yesterday. I was by Lake Galilee with my brother, mending our fishing net, when Jesus came up to us.

"Come with me," he said, "and I will make you fishers of men!"

In those days I was called Simon, but Jesus said to me, "I will call you Peter. That means 'rock'. You shall be as a rock to me, a firm and loyal friend."

My brother Andrew and I were the first of the disciples – later, more joined us, including James and John, who were fellow fishermen.

But all that happened a long time ago.

It was two days before the feast of the Passover and Jesus sent two of us to find a room where we could hold the feast.

This was always a wonderful time when we ate lamb and bread, drank wine, and remembered our ancestors' escape from Egypt, so many years ago.

But the best part of it was that we were together, all of us, friends who loved Jesus. And he loved us, of that none of us was ever in any doubt.

The feast was prepared, but as we sat Jesus said, "I tell you the truth, one of you will betray me – one who is eating with me."

I was shocked – all of us were shocked; I saw each one turn to his neighbour with a look of surprise.

Jesus had many enemies: men who were afraid of him because of his strength and his power and his goodness; men who were jealous of him for the same reason; many of the religious leaders wanted him out of the way.

But we had always guarded him, looked out for him, kept him from harm.

Jesus took the bread in his usual way and gave thanks to God. Then he passed the cup of wine among us, and went on, "You will all leave me. I am like your shepherd, and I will be struck down. And like sheep, when there is no shepherd, you will be scattered."

"Never!" I said.

"Peter," he said, "tonight, before the cock has crowed, you will say that you do not know me."

"No! Even if it meant that I should die with you, I would never do that," I cried. "I am Peter – your rock!"

But Jesus just smiled, a sad smile that troubled me.

After the feast, we all went to a place called Gethsemane. There, in the darkness of the olive grove, Jesus asked me, James and John to keep watch while he went to pray. I know that we meant to do as he asked, but one by one we fell asleep.

When Jesus came back, we awoke and felt ashamed, and did not know what to say to him. This happened three times. The third time Jesus said, "Enough. Let us go. Here is my betrayer."

And there was Judas. Judas – one of us. He came to Jesus and kissed his cheek.

As he did so a crowd of Roman soldiers with clubs and swords came rushing out from behind bushes and trees.

"Why do you come at me with clubs and swords?" Jesus said to them. "I am no rebel."

But they seized him and hurried him from the garden. In the confusion, I lost sight of the others, but I managed to follow Jesus and the soldiers at a distance. They took him to the high priest.

I was cold and shaking, and went to stand by the fire in the high priest's courtyard. As I warmed my hands a serving girl passed by me.

She stopped and stared at me. "You are one of those men who were with Jesus," she said.

"No," I said. "You are mistaken."

The words slipped from my mouth with such ease that it frightened me.

But the girl called to her friend. "Isn't this man one of the men who were with Jesus?"

Her friend looked closely at me, and nodded.

"I am not," I said.

The girls stared at me for a little longer and then left.

But as I stood a man came to stand by the fire. "Surely you are one of those who were with Jesus of Nazareth?" he said.

"No!" I said. "Leave me alone! I don't know him!"

As I spoke, the cock began to crow.

I had denied Jesus three times, just as he had said.

When I remembered his words, I crouched down and covered my face with my hands and wept. I stayed in the courtyard all night. I scarcely moved for shame and sorrow.

At first light, I saw the priests leading Jesus, whose hands were bound. They took him to Pilate, the Roman governor.

A great many people gathered outside the court, and Pilate went out to speak to them.

"It is the custom at the Passover to release a prisoner," he said. "Do you want me to release this man to you?"

But the priests moved down amongst the crowd and began to stir up feelings of fear and hatred among the people, saying, "No! Ask for Barabbas instead."

Now Barabbas, I knew, was a murderer. The crowd would not want a murderer set loose amongst them. They would ask for Jesus, the good man who cured the sick, who comforted the sad – who was innocent.

But they shouted, "Barabbas. Barabbas. Give us Barabbas!"

"And this man?" asked Pilate, turning to Jesus.

"Crucify him!" they screamed.

I heard the voices of the priests in all that great swell of angry sound.

"Crucify him! Crucify him!"

I turned away then, too sick and scared to face the crowd. I could not believe what was happening. Everything Jesus had said was coming true.

But he could not die! How would we go on without him?

Jesus was the Son of God – our teacher, our shepherd, our friend.

First Light

Illustrated by Allison Reed

When I heard the dreadful news that Jesus was to be crucified I went at once to the place. Two of my friends came with me, Joanna and another Mary. We all loved Jesus, but I had more reason to love him than most, for he cared for me, Mary Magdalene, and loved me when others did not.

They used to say of me, "The beautiful Magdalene! The proud Magdalene!"

But I am no longer proud.

And I no longer care if I am beautiful.

As we hurried along the dusty road, I told myself that we could not save him – three women could do nothing against the strength of the Roman soldiers. But I prayed that we might be allowed to ease his last hours, if only in a small way.

We were not allowed. We were not even allowed to come close, so that he might hear our voices and know that we cared. We crouched in the dusty road, and gazed up at the three crosses on the hill – for two robbers had been crucified with him, one on his left and one on his right.

The scent of the spices and ointments I had brought came up from my cloak, and I thought, Perhaps it will drift to where he is, and he will somehow know that we are here.

But no hint of our presence could have reached him, no scent, no matter how strong. Nothing, I thought, could penetrate the noise and dust raised by the Roman guards, who laughed, swore, and joked amongst themselves.

"If he is the Son of God," they said, "why doesn't he save himself?"

They shouted to him, "Come down from the cross, and save yourself!"

He didn't come down, but on the sixth hour the sky grew suddenly black. Joanna, Mary and I clung to one another, afraid. The soldiers too were afraid, I knew. They kept up their shouting and joking but it was not the same.

On the ninth hour, Jesus gave a great cry, and I knew that he had died.

The three of us went home. We did not speak, but I thought of how I had first met him, of how he had cast the devils of pride and arrogance from me. Other devils also, too terrible now to think of.

I thought of how I went to him, while he was attending a feast, and wept at his feet because I was so happy, and so grateful. I had brought a jar of precious ointment for his feet. Before I used it, I dried his feet with my long hair; I had nothing else.

I heard the voices around me. "Look how she is filled with pride!"

But Jesus said, "She is not proud – she loves," and they were silent.

And now Jesus was silent too.

It was on the third day after his death, early in the morning, when I left my home and went to find where he had been buried. A man had asked Pilate for Jesus' body, and had wrapped it in fine linen and placed it in a tomb carved out of rock. Then a great stone had been placed before the entrance.

When I reached the place I found that the stone had been rolled away and the tomb was empty. Who had taken him? And why?

I rushed back to Jerusalem to find Peter and John. They came to the tomb with me. It was true. The tomb was empty – the linen grave clothes were lying there. Peter and John were as confused as I was. They returned to the city, and I just stood there, crying.

Then I noticed a gardener standing in the distance.

I hurried to him, calling as I went, "Who has taken Jesus from his tomb? Did you see anyone? Was it the Roman guards?"

I stumbled as I ran. Then the gardener turned and said, "Mary." And I saw it was Jesus himself. He had risen, as he said he would. He was safe, and all was well. And as I stood there, in the lovely morning light, I knew that Jesus lived.

In the days that followed, many more came to know that Jesus lived. He went to his disciples soon after he had appeared to Mary Magdalene. They too were full of joy to see that he was alive.

Jesus spoke to Peter especially and asked him to take up the work that he had begun. He told them all not to worry when he was gone, for they would receive a special power from God.

Six weeks later, Jesus rose into heaven as his followers gazed up at the sky. They knew that he was truly with his father. And God sent down his spirit, so that everyone on earth might learn the story of Jesus of Nazareth.